B/RDS

THE AGHA SHAHID ALI PRIZE IN POETRY

B/RDS

Béatrice Szymkowiak

Foreword by Monica Youn

The University of Utah Press | *Salt Lake City*

AGHA SHAHID ALI

PRIZE IN POETRY

The Defiance House Man colophon is a registered trademark of the University of Utah Press. It is based on a four-foot-tall Ancient Puebloan pictograph (late PIII) near Glen Canyon, Utah.

Names: Szymkowiak, Béatrice, 1972- author. | Youn, Monica, writer of foreword.
Title: B/RDS / Béatrice Szymkowiak; with foreword by Monica Youn.
Other titles: BIRDS | Agha Shahid Ali prize in poetry.
Description: Salt Lake City : University of Utah Press, 2023. | Series: Agha Shahid Ali prize in poetry | Summary: "B/RDS endeavors to dismantle discourses that create an artificial distinction between nature and humanity through a subversive erasure of an iconic work of natural history: John James Audubon's *Birds of America* (1827-1838). This process of erasure considers the text of *Birds of America* as an archival cage. The author selectively erases words from the textual cage to reveal its ambiguity and the complex relationship between humanity and the other-than-human world. As the cage disappears, leaving a space for scarce, lyrical poems, birds break free, their voices inextricably entangled with ours. Prose poems written in the author's own words and prompted by the erasure process are also interspersed throughout the collection. These migratory poems, like ripples, trace the link between past and present and reveal the human-nature disconnect at the root cause of environmental and social problems, including the COVID-19 pandemic. Along its five movements, B/RDS also explores how we can reimagine our relationship to environment through language within new frameworks of interconnectedness. Thus, as the collection resists the distinction between nature and culture on which traditional nature poetry relies, it also acts as an ecopoetic manifesto. It suggests that a critical, lyrical poetry could contribute to ecological awareness by singing humanity back within nature"-- Provided by publisher.
Identifiers: LCCN 2023003146 | ISBN 9781647691158 (paperback) | ISBN 9781647691189 (ebook)
Subjects: LCSH: Birds--Poetry. | Birds--Migration--Poetry. | BISAC: POETRY / Subjects & Themes / Nature | POETRY / Women Authors | LCGFT: Poetry. Classification: LCC PS3619.Z964 B27 2023 | DDC 813/.6--dc23/eng/20230206
LC record available at https://lccn.loc.gov/2023003146

Cover image: *Artic Tern*, Plate CCL, from *Birds of America* by John James Audubon. Courtesy of the National Gallery of Art.

Errata and further information on this and other titles available at UofUpress.com
Printed and bound in the United State of America.

For G.

Contents

V

CODA

Foreword

In an animated television series that my son enjoys, a young boy is being chased by technologically resurrected dinosaurs. He finds the bleached skull of one of them—a velociraptor—and blows through it, sounding a resonating call so that the attacking velociraptor pack treat him as one of their own. As fantastical as this scene is, I found something about it haunting—the voice of the dead sounding a desperate call of kinship to the living, to the not-yet extinct.

Throughout Béatrice Szymkowiak's devastatingly beautiful *B/RDS*, I felt as if I were responding to a similar call, but the echoing voices in this collection are real, urgent, inescapable—a fusion of elegy and prophecy. With its trills and elisions, grace notes and percussive cries, the collection gives voice to the billions of birds lost on this continent over the past decades through human predation, industrialization, waste and sprawl—James Elroy Flecker's classic phrase seems apt: "That silence where the birds are dead / yet something pipeth like a bird."

The book alternates between lineated poems in which the words are sourced from John James Audubon's *Birds of America* and prose blocks in which the poet/speaker frees herself from the textual constraint in order to speak somewhat more directly. Szymkowiak describes Audubon's book as "a textual cage," and explains that "As the cage disappeared, birds escaped, their voices inextricably entangled with ours, a spectral, equivocal 'we.'" Where other poets often content themselves with imagining and describing catastrophe, in this collection, apocalypse resounds at the level of language itself, fracturing and stratifying and suturing it, creating grotesquely exquisite hybrids—"astonishment intermixed with grass," "tubercles of rambling dusk." There are skyscapes and there are nests, breathtakingly contingent conjunctions of softness and structure. The frequent slashes which aerate the poems serve as interfaces between animal and human, past and present, beauty and catastrophe.

As we move through the book, a narrative vector starts to emerge. Culpability coalesces around an I, associated with human rapacity. Guns and money tear apart the fragile networks of murmuration:

> I did not hear
> a single single shot.
>
> I am sorry to say.
>
> Scarcely, one / pistols

The interpenetrating choruses of call and echo diminish into a single mourning cry:

> Never nest never,
> a narrow /ing
> song/

We experience the proliferating losses from a multiplicity of perspectives, eventually resolving into scenes of a speaker and a beloved, combing a desert landscape for traces of the unremembered dead: "Crows shed dusk & you collect the fledged shadows that now drape manzanitas." This book will stay with you, will teach you to see flickering outlines in the shadows, to hear the echo of wingbeats in the desolate breezes. In the imminent unthinkable future, will it be any consolation if all our swan songs are as beautiful as this?

— Monica Youn

Preface

B/RDS is part of an investigation into the new environmental trajectory of the Anthropocene and our relationship with the other-than-human world. The project is focused on *Birds of America* (1827-1838)—J. J. Audubon's iconic ornithological and archival work. Knowing that North America has lost three billion birds since 1970 (*Science,* 2019) inspired a process of lyrical erasure and reflection, to question disconnected epistemological approaches to the other-than-human world, including that of natural history and its urge to archive nature.

My writing process started by considering the text of *Birds of America* (the *Ornithological Biography* accompanying the drawings) as an archival cage. For this reason, I resolved to strictly abide by the rule of keeping the order of the words (or letters) from the text-source—my text-source being *Birds of America* in alphabetical order. I then selectively erased the textual cage to reveal its ambiguity and the complex relationship between humanity and the other-than-human world. As the cage disappeared, birds escaped, their voices inextricably entangled with ours—a spectral, equivocal "we." Finally, I reshuffled the resulting poems and added migratory poems written in my own words and prompted by lines from the erasure poems. These migratory poems, like ripples, trace the link between past and present.

We want to touch the sky. Speak as if sum of *us* / some of *us*. Presumptuous, arrogant little cheat—*I & impostures*. Are *we* m/other dirt? Compass / trespass. *You & me & you &*　　　　　*them*? Plural singularity. Winged / wingless. *We* metamorphose. Touch, tangle, terrify each other/s neck to neck intimate / love song disconnect / DID (Dissociative Identity Disorder) connect. Pyric, spectral. Microbiota imbroglio. *Hold |me| together.* Dance performance. Animal magnetism. Let our wishbone break / the cage —Oh but the fall. Who is what is who? Fe/male, dirt, b/rd, d/earth. *You & I &, &, &.*　　　　*Us*

B/RDS

"It was then that the authors of all this devastation began their entry amongst the dead, the dying, and the mangled." —J. J. Audubon

Along Shallow & Grassy Shores

A would-be poet carves our tongues
with a quill. Songs skulk around

our necks, as grooves ramble
into strange notes / mistaken

for migration or another new
world. The motions of the feather

perform in flesh-color ink
the act of flying / we fall from.

I

Around the Heavens

We moved in silence, well-spread
wings flapping dusk and low

in search for the beginning of March.
We found the reverse / inflected

elliptical, outer curved outwards
towards their factories of belief.

We were wishes of elm or holly /
abbreviated. We were breeds

with claws resembling a human nail.

It Is Nothing but a Song

A tongue, twilight
of clouded season,

nests pensive in blue
mandible edged with slit—

larynx toward horizon.

Viscera

The abandoned sticks of hour cling
to claws. We wait until *farewell the orb*

devours our last /ing. Sunrise, again
sunset mingled in ploughed earth, yields

tubercles of rambling dusk. How hunger
hobbles the graceful notes / we feign

midsummer warble with bluish angle,
sing evergreens / ascending solitude.

Sunset Mingled in Ploughed Earth, Yields

Numbers. A horizon bleeds a sun splayed into nebula. Radio statics spit *odd opacities* & the day dies all over our windshield, the Platte River Valley dwindled into smoldering ponds. Our eyes becloud over flooded farmlands until *fluid leaks from tiny vessels* fields suddenly heave into air, darken the sky. A million geese migrating across equinox, have convened night *after lungs collapse* & will carry us through to where light mists the last frost.

The Trembling

Over meadows & rivers, across tail
feathers, wanting. A cluster of live

oaks. Along salt water ponds
or swamps. In mangroves, cedars,

cypresses. From throbbing wounds,
from night's ruffles. Oh, necks.

Over meadows & rivers, an echo,
tails, fleeting. A lively sough

through oak leaves. Above marshes
or mires. Across tussocks,

clearings, plains. From open
wounds, along necks, oh arched

into night. Over meadows & rivers,
through air. Above oak, gasping

in slough. By fields or fences. Oh,
from rotten wounds, from longing

necks. Suddenly, ceased.

Gnawings

A wide estuary, a grassy instance,
remain with us / all imaginable

like a hatch of light. Some fly
against beacons & lighthouses,

some plunge towards the bottom
of shallow rains / Others lie

on shore until they turn to grass.
The night is pitch-dark but we /

shiver the impossible day out
of drifted dawn & small twigs.

The Night Is Pitch-Dark but We /

murmur through shattered glass *breathe, breathe, the light from dead stars still glows!* Along night eaves, mangled starlings heave stellar wings to tenebrous ceilings & tilt equinox back to *breathe, breathe* constellations. *Light* is shattered *from the* mangled night. How many *dead stars still glow?* Tenebrous wings cleave away *from* you, heave equinox back to pitch-dark ceilings. *Breathe, breathe,* starlings murmur along mangled eaves, how constellations tilt *from dead stars* to *light! Still* you, shattered wings through tenebrous glass murmur how many, how many *dead stars*

                                  & cleave equinox halves away.

Re/sound

How pleasing when a clouded sky
ripens with rain. Water-logged

seeds imagine blossoms & the swell
of duration / wings sail along

ponds & hedges / clear rivulets
root rivers. Hear in shallow pools,

the unremitted flappings / flocks
wading the course of days

in the afterstorm / an axe's thud
hung at the extremity of a twig

drops & drowns. Rings ripple,
quills / fly off.

How Far South It May Be

Half-closed wings fold
horizon into storm /

fading away from us.
We scratch earth for gales

choked to rocks, gather
their oval chests

like m/others mourning
the swiftness of meteors.

We imagine air,
the velocity of thousands.

The Latter Part of Autumn

Our number /equal to that of the falling
leaves of the trees in places writhed by

imagine taking flight / is falling. Cages
swing light & remiss. The ground beneath

sinks as nightfall / rots in abundance
of berries. We cannot conceive

a single wing / passing over
a meadow / plunge headlong

towards the Earth,
that trembles.

II

American Co.

I did not hear
a single single shot.

I am sorry to say.

Scarcely, one / pistols

The Winged Lovers

were killed outright.

Their arched tongues & sea
salt mouths.

The merry little song, along
their bare breasts.

The flood of golden light,
bending.

Their so tender necks.
Oh, the tearing & rapture.

The sickle of sorrow.

A /complete History

In early autumn, on high sandy hills
on an island on the coast, it was dawn,
and the fog, and the fog.

The density of mist, the heavy gales,
rocks here & there. Oh, but the course,
from sunrise to sunset.

Skirting the forests, w/ere a fellow,
a f/iend, winter rushed forth, winter
& the lords of hours.

Fierce sticks & stakes / once hunger
satisfied, it was not. And they preyed,
and they preyed.

Spring hovering over us / split in their
mouths / trees, streams, and the air,
gulped.

A black/dashed orb rolled down
high sandy hills / it was night,
and the dark / and the dark.

Fierce Sticks & Stakes / Once Hunger

guts sleep, you spit spikes, comb them into feathers *In ancient Rome, people would nail an owl* until air softens *to their door* & I unstring our bones from fearful necks, *to ward off evil* reinvent amulets into furcula. When you suddenly wake out of night sockets, you see without beyond: we are not grim auguries, neither convenient evil. Only four wings unstitched from the sky.

Spring Was the Thickness of a Dollar

Banks of seize them snatch them.

Holes for the purpose.

Bank of ground, bank of bluffs.

Little winged holes, day after day.

Banks of depth suffocate.

Banks of small bits, devour 'em, cont'd.

Bones of no purpose / ruff red,

harbinger of Summer seldom.

How Bodies with Wings

dive stark mad into the night /
the newly fallen, muzzled

like humbled barbarians.
In search of pasture /

we found putrid fish, their
eyes honeyed with ethereal

beings. We dreamed
zig-zags into sky, loud

latitudes & wildly /
dove back to dusk.

Sans Doute l'Oiseau

Or want or rage
              / or their cries.

Claws into innards, we crowd clear

blue heaven
        with protruding tongues /

                feu-de-joie
vociferating

breast-shots & huddled terrors

                    to /selves.

The Instant They Are Caught,
They Are Wont to Mute

ob/

obl/

obt/

/ack

/ack

op/

/ack

opp/

ov/

Hem/locks

Wing whirling within
twig twig sorrow log.
Never nest never,
a narrow /ing
song/

     Where
where does not go
beyond air in that
seven or eight,
six in/

     Tangled
dangling glance.
Remember solitudes
bellow louder, twig
twig tortuous neck
singly clench   tw/

III

Confinement Notes

Rusty hinges & blunt claws grate
our small attachments. An ache

moth records cuttings / the salt
of sea tales, in which drift wood

holds time. Shell fragments fill
the bottom of cavities. We lie

among dead journeys & conjure
isthmus to cross silence.

On the beach, muddy pools
collect evening's coolness,

until night & mangroves
take us / one by one /

brackish eyes dissolving
locks / limbs unraveled

in emerald-green farewell.

Our Small Attachments. An Ache

The hour keel spins along the grooves her voice hovers. *Dearest, the shadows* pool in your chest. You pour yourself a Dark & Stormy, the Mississippi River bends around the mid-century chair you sink in. Lady Day sings a blue bird & outside, it still snows. Above you, the lamp shade leaks a muddled sun endless, wrecks.

In the Interior

Our bodies gravel at times / fragments
of minute shells. Distant songs / rise

from the barrens, or is it / creaking noise?
We do not fret / light, but the knowing

& its amphitheater / to be caught alive
in a wax wing act. Thus we still, sylph

stunted buds & heed in the distance
choruses chanting / Spring's return.

Spring along the Ridge

Are we their cries dislocated
from the beginning of March

shot alit? Love-season
grows on tongues

infected with desire
of streams, im/memorial.

Hear the rattling notes / our
cascades disgorged

into salt water refrain.
Twig twig, rocky shores,

wherever sun ends
in the straits of throat.

Wherever Sun Ends

Two crows perched in the pine grove caw ghosts of unsung passing. Ice spears from the eaves. Dread devours clouds. I fear how tangible your tongue before its silence. Deer ellipses dot the snow thawing clock. On the ground, a red-tailed hawk claws & tears its own disappearance.

Humanity Fills /our Hearts

with loose sand & elsewhere.
At three o'clock, it is twelve

& we specter, until driven off
by tide, or the appearance of

flesh. Fortunate mortal, dead
fish float. We, but tenacious

carnage, fly south, breasts
dispersed into new shores.

Cleft

Ever-craving we other / they
elapse. A wide fissure

was found shivering by the lee
of a rock. More were seen

nesting side by side,
together w/hole

on the shore. Gullet
cluster of mere /lack nights.

The Higher

Tide ebbs & our bones
whiten the shore. Inland,

offal rots on / the broken
stones of shrines. Oil slick

shells remind gods / of wings
& botched sacrifice / they fast

forget. Sea rises. Flows rattle
a strange alabaster crop.

Stones of Shrines. Oil Slick

A solid sky, a lake frozen in its heave exhales dry ice. Nothing but the exhausts of winter hardening our wings, swan figurehead puncturing snow from Summer paddleboats. The geese have gone, honked their way through air traffic, taunting the bells immured in their towers. Concrete stills our vestigial wishbones.

Becalmed

As if by way of resting,
we lie so close as almost

to touch. The sea riddles
in the bay / memory of /

a world now sunk in
seaweeds. We gently

crawl to the water,
for a moment then,

ample & indistinct.

IV

Decree of Shyness

I shot the remainder, shot
its movements until /

shot little more, scarcely
a quantity / I have never

/ever spread their wings
transverse on sticks /

without a cry.

The Natural History Society

dreams ventriloquy & dissection,
gizzards filled with *what voracious*

creatures they are! Judge-mandibles
congratulating themselves

as possessed of Divine, they draw
the long blade & gut the nests

macerated in their extended throats.

The Only Authentic Account

Imagine what you see /

Territories & the coldest
part of winter. They

at all times they, heavens.
Downwards from the tree-tops!

    / Cut of/

Bucketful of bluish. The bluer /
the tamer.

Neck, neck / at ease,
as if afterlife.

Log to log, come-to-me.

Nowhere / into a thicket.
Mystery rendez-vous.

How wonderful!

Lasts.

A Prize! A Prize!

A New American Fauna

This species from open woods / with blades.

This species as long as it sings.

This species / accidentally.

This species grass grass again/st.

This species nothing better / than skin.

This species as proof.

This species through glass.

This species never before never before.

This species scratching /earth.

This species from wished-for-land.

This species at the approach of night.

This species / but the next.

This species when well cooked.

This species from sorrow log.

This species speci/men.

This species of withered reed.

This species all creatures / all pleasures.

This species from the dried twigs at the extremity of a branch.

This species / south.

This species as if by magic.

This species in a single evening.

This species / dead sticks.

Exhibit

February & dry twigs. We were
not what we had supposed /

the motion of alders, a spruce top,
the air enabled, that / possibility /

killed and put in spirits. We floated,
cold fog of sedated wor/ds,

under a same name. To the end
of tail, 14 1/8 inches.

Ma/rion/ette

The head can rise / as if glee
could fly out of their throats /

as if exceeding departure.
When raised / wings decurved

from dusk to blossoms, compass
migrations di/splayed as sinew

yonder & rustling breeze.

Migrations Di/splayed as Sinew

Which pair of shoes? My hand caresses the leather, once innervated skin.
We know too well how to evacuate: *essentials* packed, you drive first.
Roadkill hawks peer from fence posts at flayed squirrels to scavenge. We
flee from hotel to hotel to elsewhere. We know too well the rooms are
strange. On a neat corner bed, belongings overflow from butterflied
suitcases we peer at. My silence brushes yours. I forgot my *Red Wing* boots.

As if Bewildered

we
sc/
rat/
ch
the
ca/
ge
un/
til
we
dis/
    appear

Identified Trace Specimen

Alleged brownish-black tail passes
and repasses the rugged shores,

      in part / true, voraciously

blossoms of full-fledged earth

         —reported darker

and hurriedly off.

Papillae

Spurs

      of huddle

         alula / we

w/ere /ours

      upward fl/

          & they

V

Of Be/coming

An eclipse now roosts beneath our wings.
We hear wolves howl & the monosyllables

of an axe. Trees are felled, then named.
We compose clocks with sticks, hang them

around our necks / forget the old elm,
that would gnarl wood into wishes. Maps

peel off from beech logs. We mask
with torn legends & act *l'orée du bois*

as a clearing. When fog moans through
the forest / a cage is lit to guide our path.

We vanish, deer blossom.

Blades of Grass

Forgetful dancers bloom
out of their breasts / as if

they were brothers, perform
the impossible escape beyond

which / we found ourselves,
monsters of granite crumbling

down the morrows. There / we are
astonishment intermixed with grass,

gleaning among willows
for the beginning of March.

Out of their Breasts / as if

I found a bird skull blooming in an oak grove like a plague doctor's mask, its beak scented with piñon & juniper. Death is discarnate in the desert. Crows shed dusk & you collect the fledged shadows that now drape manzanitas. My fingers brush skeletal trees, fumbling for the flesh of residual rain. I meet you in the penumbra, murmur *light* from the first point of Aries.

We almost Touched Each Other

By the rushing waters of a brook /
off a cliff.

Sharp tooth-like / skinned
in trap-cages.

To cross was to dis/possess
the azure. We / would always fail.

Imagined memory of confluence /
in the Gallery of the Louvre.

To cross was to monarch wings
& enclose / sky /

in our imminence.

Notwithstanding

That the fact of our being has become un/deniable.
That they cut the blade near the roo/t.
That we cling to reeds / neck erect.
That they whistle /civilities & shift
                    from one hill to another.
That we remain.
That we, by a perfect stillness.
That twigs elapse & when least
        expected / the crossing in thousand /ways.
That wings, tongues, sternums.
That intermingled we / they
                    unsteady flickering.
That wound & that nothing

is known, but the /heft.

A/part

When utter/ed time. When half
reaches, but never. Rock / head /

rock. *Oh, the trimming.* When after
extends night / crowd of severed

tongues, a discontinuity / occurs
along the river. Water parts

into ground rain. Thunder rumbles
with intrusion. Here, we enter silence

inhabited by the length of a neck,
wanting.

Tongues, a Discontinuity / Occurs

Around the picnic table, a plague of grackles pecks our words a nameless wind dispelled. We sit at six feet from each other, wonder about the anonymous "dead horse" the park is called. A few scavengers ruffle their feathers, shriek Spring from nightfall. We discuss our uneasiness of crowds, birdsong mnemonics & cottonwood snow. The dark flock soars, squalls. We cannot remember how to

As Blossoms Fade

We move in truth, tangled
& barbarous / begging

for a mouth of breathless
river to swallow us, finally

whole. Our ardent song,
rudely woven & coarse,

hangs on a fish-hook,
dangles in rotten reeds.

We plead wind, we plead
frogs & water-lizards, let us

sink into quick-streams,
with the grace of one

/ drowned rose.

Whole. Our Ardent Song

Half feathers half gnawed a gull thaws out of its ice carcass. Debacle teases, thwarts its embankment, wings half floe half loose dangle in the currents. How long have we been here, bent over the bridge railing? Your frozen fingers point to a flailing tangle, as if a gull you look at me, half sunken half

To the Water That Carries Them Gently

Fill the roof of their mouths
with root songs & mosses,

but leave their winter dress,
a vivid red, trace the sill

of broken windows,
as they enter the river.

Collect their sunset
& ignite the course

towards our self
immolation.

CODA

The Remembrance of Thousands

Twig, twig, be/loved. A field of quivering c/lover & there, perched on a fence-stake / adieu boughs & mosses. B/orders breed through the night. Wings hatch from blades of grass, cleave. An/other, an/other. Note louder than a love-call / perched on a fence-stake. Adieu gentle, as if Spring or Autumn. / The hatchets have mangled the last pines deaf / a chattering unsettles, flocks after flocks.

Acknowledgements

This book would never have been completed without the unwavering and loving support of my wife, Nicole Taylor. Thank you for always being by my side, reading my work, and believing in me.

Thank you also to Brenda Cárdenas, for her kindness, her insights, and for supporting this project from its inception and throughout; to Kyce Bello, whose thoughtful remarks helped improve the latest versions of *B/RDS*; and to Joan Naviyuk Kane and Sherwin Bitsui who invited me to join their classes to present *B/RDS* as it was still in process.

The poem "Spring Was the Thickness of a Dollar" was published in *Sycamore Review,* issue 32.1, 2021. "Around the Heavens," "It Is Nothing but a Song," and "American Co." were published in *Terrain.org*, November 19, 2020. "Viscera," "Blades of Grass," and "Of Be/coming" were published in *Inverted Syntax*, November 2022. Thank you to their editors for seeing my work.